Frog and Toad Together

A guide for the book by Arnold Lobel
Great Works Author: Emily R. Smith

SHELL EDUCATION

Publishing Credits

Robin Erickson, *Production Director*; Lee Aucoin, *Creative Director*;
Timothy J. Bradley, *Illustration Manager*; Emily R. Smith, M.A.Ed., *Editorial Director*; Amber Goff, *Editorial Assistant*; Don Tran, *Production Supervisor*;
Corinne Burton, M.A.Ed., *Publisher*

Image Credits

Cover and interior illustrations by Timothy J. Bradley and Stephanie Reid McGinley
Other images from Shutterstock

Standards

© 2007 Teachers of English to Speakers of Other Languages, Inc. (TESOL)
© 2007 Board of Regents of the University of Wisconsin System. World-Class Instructional Design and Assessment (WIDA)
© Copyright 2010. National Governors Association Center for Best Practices and Council of Chief State School Officers.
All rights reserved.

Shell Education

5301 Oceanus Drive
Huntington Beach, CA 92649-1030
http://www.shelleducation.com
ISBN 978-1-4258-8964-7
© 2014 Shell Educational Publishing, Inc.

Table of contents

How to Use This Literature Guide

Today's standards demand rigor and relevance in the reading of complex texts. The units in this series guide teachers in a rich and deep exploration of worthwhile works of literature for classroom study. The most rigorous instruction can also be interesting and engaging!

Many current strategies for effective literacy instruction have been incorporated into these instructional guides for literature. Throughout the units, text-dependent questions are used to determine comprehension of the book as well as student interpretation of the vocabulary words. The books chosen for the series are complex and are exemplars of carefully crafted works of literature. Close reading is used throughout the units to guide students toward revisiting the text and using textual evidence to respond to prompts orally and in writing. Students must analyze the story elements in multiple assignments for each section of the book. All of these strategies work together to rigorously guide students through their study of literature.

The next few pages will make clear how to use this guide for a purposeful and meaningful literature study. Each section of this guide is set up in the same way to make it easier for you to implement the instruction in your classroom.

Theme Thoughts

The great works of literature used throughout this series have important themes that have been relevant to people for many years. Many of the themes will be discussed during the various sections of this instructional guide. However, it would also benefit students to have independent time to think about the key themes of the book.

Before students begin reading, have them complete the *Pre-Reading Theme Thoughts* (page 13). This graphic organizer will allow students to think about the themes outside the context of the story. They'll have the opportunity to evaluate statements based on important themes and defend their opinions. Be sure to keep students' papers for comparison to the *Post-Reading Theme Thoughts* (page 59). This graphic organizer is similar to the pre-reading activity. However, this time, students will be answering the questions from the point of view of one of the characters in the book. They have to think about how the character would feel about each statement and defend their thoughts. To conclude the activity, have students compare what they thought about the themes before the book to what the characters discovered during the story.

How to Use This Literature Guide (cont.)

Vocabulary

Each teacher reference vocabulary overview page has definitions and sentences about how key vocabulary words are used in the section. These words should be introduced and discussed with students. Students will use these words in different activities throughout the book.

On some of the vocabulary student pages, students are asked to answer text-related questions about vocabulary words from the sections. The following question stems will help you create your own vocabulary questions if you'd like to extend the discussion.

- How does this word describe _____'s character?
- How does this word connect to the problem in this story?
- How does this word help you understand the setting?
- Tell me how this word connects to the main idea of this story.
- What visual pictures does this word bring to your mind?
- Why do you think the author used this word?

At times, you may find that more work with the words will help students understand their meanings and importance. These quick vocabulary activities are a good way to further study the words.

- Students can play vocabulary concentration. Make one set of cards that have the words on them and another set with the definitions. Then, have students lay them out on the table and play concentration. The goal of the game is to match vocabulary words with their definitions. For early readers or English language learners, the sets of cards could be the words and pictures of the words.
- Students can create word journal entries about the words. Students choose words they think are important and then describe why they think each word is important within the book. Early readers or English language learners could instead draw pictures about the words in a journal.
- Students can create puppets and use them to act out the vocabulary words from the stories. Artwork of the characters is provided on pages 61–63. Students can use these images to retell the stories using the vocabulary words. Students may also enjoy using the artwork to tell their own character-driven stories using vocabulary words from the original stories.

How to Use This Literature Guide (cont.)

Analyzing the Literature

After you have read each section with students, hold a small-group or whole-class discussion. Provided on the teacher reference page for each section are leveled questions. The questions are written at two levels of complexity to allow you to decide which questions best meet the needs of your students. The Level 1 questions are typically less abstract than the Level 2 questions. These questions are focused on the various story elements, such as character, setting, and plot. Be sure to add further questions as your students discuss what they've read. For each question, a few key points are provided for your reference as you discuss the book with students.

Reader Response

In today's classrooms, there are often great readers who are below average writers. So much time and energy is spent in classrooms getting students to read on grade level that little time is left to focus on writing skills. To help teachers include more writing in their daily literacy instruction, each section of this guide has a literature-based reader response prompt. Each of the three genres of writing is used in the reader responses within this guide: narrative, informative/explanatory, and opinion. Before students write, you may want to allow them time to draw pictures related to the topic. Book-themed writing paper is provided on pages 69–70 if your students need more space to write.

Guided Close Reading

Within each section of this guide, it is suggested that you closely reread a portion of the text with your students. Page numbers are given, but since some versions of the books may have different page numbers, the sections to be reread are described by location as well. After rereading the section, there are a few text-dependent questions to be answered by students. A graphic organizer has been provided to help students prepare for the group discussion. They should record their thoughts and ideas on the graphic organizer and refer to it during your discussion. If your students are working above grade level, you may want to encourage them to respond to the questions in complete sentences.

Encourage students to read one question at a time and then go back to the text and discover the answer. Work with students to ensure that they use the text to determine their answers rather than making unsupported inferences. Suggested answers are provided in the answer key.

How to Use This Literature Guide *(cont.)*

Guided Close Reading *(cont.)*

The generic open-ended stems below can be used to write your own text-dependent questions if you would like to give students more practice.

- What words in the story support . . . ?
- What text helps you understand . . . ?
- Use the book to tell why _____ happens.
- Based on the events in the story, . . . ?
- Show me the part in the text that supports . . . .
- Use the text to tell why . . . .

Making Connections

The activities in this section help students make cross-curricular connections to mathematics, science, social studies, fine arts, or other curricular areas. These activities require higher-order thinking skills from students but also allow for creative thinking.

Language Learning

A special section has been set aside to connect the literature to language conventions. Through these activities, students will have opportunities to practice the conventions of standard English grammar, usage, capitalization, and punctuation.

Story Elements

It is important to spend time discussing what the common story elements are in literature. Understanding the characters, setting, plot, and theme can increase students' comprehension and appreciation of the story. If teachers begin discussing these elements in early childhood, students will more likely internalize the concepts and look for the elements in their independent reading. Another very important reason for focusing on the story elements is that students will be better writers if they think about how the stories they read are constructed.

In the story elements activities, students are asked to create work related to the characters, setting, or plot. Consider having students complete only one of these activities. If you give students a choice on this assignment, each student can decide to complete the activity that most appeals to him or her. Different intelligences are used so that the activities are diverse and interesting to all students.

How to Use This Literature Guide (cont.)

Culminating Activity

At the end of this instructional guide is a creative culminating activity that allows students the opportunity to share what they've learned from reading the book. This activity is open ended so that students can push themselves to create their own great works within your language arts classroom.

Comprehension Assessment

The questions in this section require students to think about the book they've read as well as the words that were used in the book. Some questions are tied to quotations from the book to engage students and require them to think about the text as they answer the questions.

Response to Literature

Finally, students are asked to respond to the literature by drawing pictures and writing about the characters and stories. A suggested rubric is provided for teacher reference.

Correlation to the Standards

Shell Education is committed to producing educational materials that are research and standards based. In this effort, we have correlated all of our products to the academic standards of all 50 United States, the District of Columbia, the Department of Defense Dependents Schools, and all Canadian provinces.

Purpose and Intent of Standards

Standards are designed to focus instruction and guide adoption of curricula. Standards are statements that describe the criteria necessary for students to meet specific academic goals. They define the knowledge, skills, and content students should acquire at each level. Standards are also used to develop standardized tests to evaluate students' academic progress. Teachers are required to demonstrate how their lessons meet standards. Standards are used in the development of all of our products, so educators can be assured they meet high academic standards.

How To Find Standards Correlations

To print a customized correlation report of this product for your state, visit our website at http://www.shelleducation.com and follow the online directions. If you require assistance in printing correlation reports, please contact Customer Service at 1-877-777-3450.

correlation to the standards (cont.)

standards correlation chart

The lessons in this guide were written to support the Common Core College and Career Readiness Anchor Standards. This chart indicates which sections of this guide address the anchor standards.

Common Core College and Career Readiness Anchor Standard	Section
CCSS.ELA-Literacy.CCRA.R.1—Read closely to determine what the text says explicitly and to make logical inferences from it; cite specific textual evidence when writing or speaking to support conclusions drawn from the text.	Guided Close Reading Sections 1–5; Story Elements Section 1
CCSS.ELA-Literacy.CCRA.R.2—Determine central ideas or themes of a text and analyze their development; summarize the key supporting details and ideas.	Theme Thoughts; Analyzing the Literature Sections 1–5; Story Elements Sections 1–5
CCSS.ELA-Literacy.CCRA.R.3—Analyze how and why individuals, events, or ideas develop and interact over the course of a text.	Analyzing the Literature Sections 1–5; Guided Close Reading Sections 1–5; Story Elements Sections 3, 5
CCSS.ELA-Literacy.CCRA.R.4—Interpret words and phrases as they are used in a text, including determining technical, connotative, and figurative meanings, and analyze how specific word choices shape meaning or tone.	Vocabulary Sections 1–5
CCSS.ELA-Literacy.CCRA.R.5—Analyze the structure of texts, including how specific sentences, paragraphs, and larger portions of the text (e.g., a section, a chapter) relate to each other and the whole.	Analyzing the Literature Sections 1–5
CCSS.ELA-Literacy.CCRA.R.10—Read and comprehend complex literary and informational texts independently and proficiently.	Entire Unit
CCSS.ELA-Literacy.CCRA.W.1—Write arguments to support claims in an analysis of substantive topics or texts, using valid reasoning and relevant and sufficient evidence.	Reader Response Section 2; Post-Reading Response to Literature
CCSS.ELA-Literacy.CCRA.W.2—Write informative/explanatory texts to examine and convey complex ideas and information clearly and accurately through the effective selection, organization, and analysis of content.	Reader Response Sections 3, 5; Post-Reading Response to Literature
CCSS.ELA-Literacy.CCRA.W.3—Write narratives to develop real or imagined experiences or events using effective technique, well-chosen details and well-structured event sequences.	Reader Response Sections 1, 4

correlation to the Standards (cont.)

Standards correlation chart (cont.)

Common Core College and Career Readiness Anchor Standard	Section
CCSS.ELA-Literacy.CCRA.W.4—Produce clear and coherent writing in which the development, organization, and style are appropriate to task, purpose, and audience.	Making Connections Sections 1–2; Story Elements Section 2; Post-Reading Response to Literature
CCSS.ELA-Literacy.CCRA.L.1—Demonstrate command of the conventions of standard English grammar and usage when writing or speaking.	Reader Response Sections 1–5; Language Learning Sections 1, 3–4; Post-Reading Response to Literature
CCSS.ELA-Literacy.CCRA.L.2—Demonstrate command of the conventions of standard English capitalization, punctuation, and spelling when writing.	Reader Response Sections 1–5; Language Learning Sections 2, 5; Post-Reading Response to Literature
CCSS.ELA-Literacy.CCRA.L.4—Determine or clarify the meaning of unknown and multiple-meaning words and phrases by using context clues, analyzing meaningful word parts, and consulting general and specialized reference materials as appropriate.	Vocabulary Sections 1–5
CCSS.ELA-Literacy.CCRA.L.6—Acquire and use accurately a range of general academic and domain-specific words and phrases sufficient for reading, writing, speaking, and listening at the college and career readiness level; demonstrate independence in gathering vocabulary knowledge when encountering an unknown term important to comprehension or expression.	Vocabulary Sections 1–5

TESOL and WIDA Standards

The lessons in this book promote English language development for English language learners. The following TESOL and WIDA English Language Development Standards are addressed through the activities in this book:

- **Standard 1:** English language learners communicate for social and instructional purposes within the school setting.

- **Standard 2:** English language learners communicate information, ideas and concepts necessary for academic success in the content area of language arts.

About the Author—Arnold Lobel

Arnold Lobel was born on May 22, 1933, in Los Angeles, California. He grew up in Schenectady, New York. As a young boy, Lobel enjoyed reading and drawing. He attended art school and married Anita Kempler, who was also a children's illustrator.

Once he graduated, Lobel began to work in advertising. He did not enjoy working in that environment. However, there were not very many successful children's authors yet. Lobel decided to try illustrating children's books. After many visits to publishers, Harper and Row gave him a chance. After a while, he began writing books to better support his family financially.

Lobel stated in multiple interviews that he was not very confident about his writing. However, he was confident in his artistic ability. His work was first published in 1958, and he continued to be published until he died in 1987. His daughter, Adrianna, pulled together books of his work that have been published posthumously.

In 1981, he won the Caldecott Medal for *Fables*, which he authored and illustrated. His 1972 book, *Frog and Toad Together*, is a Newbery Award Honor book. *Frog and Toad Are Friends* is a Caldecott Award Honor book.

Possible Texts for Text comparisons

There are three other books in this Arnold Lobel series: *Frog and Toad Are Friends*; *Frog and Toad All Year*; and *Days with Frog and Toad*. *Mouse Tales* and *Mouse Soup* may also be used for enriching text comparisons by the same author.

Book Summary of *Frog and Toad Together*

Friendship is an important concept to discuss with young learners. It is a part of their lives every day and affects how they perceive themselves. One of the best-known book series on friendship is Arnold Lobel's four Frog and Toad books. In these books, two best friends have adventures and enjoy spending time with each other in a variety of situations. *Frog and Toad Together* is the second book in the series. It was published in 1972 and is a Newbery Honor book.

In *Frog and Toad Together*, five different stories introduce readers to the value of friendship.

- In "A List," Toad creates a list of what he would like to accomplish in a day. He enjoys the feeling he gets when he crosses items off of his list. On a walk with Frog, his list is lost. Toad feels helpless. Luckily, Frog is there to support his friend.

- In "The Garden," Toad wants to plant a garden as beautiful as Frog's garden. He tries many different ways to help his seeds grow. Finally, after a little sun and rain, the seeds begin to sprout. Frog and Toad celebrate together.

- Toad bakes some delicious treats in "Cookies." Unfortunately, Frog and Toad can't seem to find any will power. They just keep eating the cookies! Frog eventually solves the problem.

- "Dragons and Giants" is a funny story about bravery. Frog and Toad think they're brave, but after an adventurous day together, they end up hiding in Toad's house talking about being brave.

- In "The Dream," Toad imagines himself outshining Frog. As Toad does better and better, Frog grows smaller and smaller. Toad gets scared about losing his best friend and wakes up to find Frog standing by his bed ready for the day.

Cross-Curricular Connection

This book can be used in a science unit on the study of amphibians or in a social studies unit on civil behavior and getting along.

Possible Texts for Text Sets

- Clarke, Barry. *DK Eyewitness Books: Amphibians*. DK Children, 2005.
- Gibbons, Gail, *Frogs*. Holiday House, 1994.
- Rice, Dona Herweck. *A Frog's Life*. Teacher Created Materials, 2011.

or

- dePaola, Tomie. *Bill and Pete*. Puffin, 1996.
- Keller, Holly. *Help! A Story of Friendship*. Greenwillow Books, 2007.
- Kellogg, Steven. *Best Friends*. Puffin, 1992.

Name _____

Pre-Reading Theme Thoughts

Directions: Draw a picture of a happy face or a sad face. Your face should show how you feel about each statement. Then, use words to say what you think about each statement.

Statement	How Do You Feel? ☺ ☹	What Do You Think?
Best friends should help each other.		
It is important to be patient. That means you have to wait for good things to happen.		
Sometimes you have to stop doing something you love.		
You have to be brave when you're scared.		

Vocabulary Overview

Key words and phrases from this section are provided below with definitions and sentences about how the words are used in the story. Introduce and discuss these important vocabulary words with students. If you think these words or other words in the story warrant more time devoted to them, there are suggestions in the introduction for other vocabulary activities (page 5).

Word	Definition	Sentence about Text
frog (cover)	a tailless amphibian with long back legs and moist skin	One of the main characters in this book is a **frog**.
toad (cover)	a tailless amphibian with short back legs and dry skin	The other main character in this book is a **toad**.
together (cover)	to be near each other; not alone	Frog and Toad spend a lot of time **together**.
list (pg. 1)	to put things in order	At the beginning of the story, Toad makes a **list** of what he plans to do.
remember (pg. 4)	to use your memory to think about something	Toad hopes that the list will help him **remember** what to do.
piece (pg. 4)	one thing out of a collection or group	Toad uses one **piece** of paper to create his list.
crossed out (pg. 5)	to remove from a list	Toad draws a line through, or **crosses out**, each task as he completes it.
knocked (p. 10)	to hit against something with your hand	When Toad arrives at Frog's house, he **knocks** on the door.
blowing (pg. 13)	moving air	The wind is **blowing** Toad's list around.
swamps (pg. 15)	areas of low land that flood every year	Frog runs across hills and **swamps** chasing Toad's lost list.

Name _____

Vocabulary Activity

Directions: Choose at least two words from the story. Draw a picture that shows what these words mean. Label your picture.

Words from the Story

frog	toad	together	list	remember
piece	crossed out	knocked	swamps	blowing

Directions: Answer this question.

1. Who loses his **list** in this story?

_____

- - - - - - - - - - - - - - - - -

_____

Analyzing the Literature

Provided below are discussion questions you can use in small groups, with the whole class, or for written assignments. Each question is written at two levels so you can choose the right question for each group of students. For each question, a few key points are provided for your reference as you discuss the book with students.

Story Element	Level 1	Level 2	Key Discussion Points
Character	How do you know that Frog is a good friend?	In what ways does Frog support Toad in the story?	Frog immediately goes on a walk when Toad suggests it. Frog takes a long walk with Toad. Frog runs after the list even when Toad won't. Frog sits for a long time with Toad trying to figure out what to do about the lost list. Frog goes to sleep with Toad.
Plot	What is the problem in this story?	Describe multiple problems in this story.	The list blows away, and Toad doesn't know what to do. There is also the problem that Toad can't move past losing his list. He needs to figure out a way to continue with his day even though he doesn't have his list anymore.
Setting	What is the most interesting part of the setting of the book?	Describe the setting of the story.	The story takes place near Frog and Toad's houses. They also take a long walk and sit on a hill as they wait toward the end of the day. Students should use the pictures to gather information about the setting.
Plot	Who solves Toad's problem?	In what ways does the story's solution not really solve any problems?	Toad solves his own problem when he remembers that he had "Go to sleep" on his list. However, the problem still exists when Toad wakes up. Students may realize that Frog and Toad will still have to face the problem later.

Name _____

Reader Response

Think

In "A List," Toad writes a list. Think about a time when you wrote a list. Did the list help you?

Narrative Writing Prompt

Write about a time that you used a list in your own life.

_____

- - - - - - - - - - - - - - - - - - - -

_____

- - - - - - - - - - - - - - - - - - - -

_____

_____

- - - - - - - - - - - - - - - - - - - -

_____

_____

- - - - - - - - - - - - - - - - - - - -

_____

- - - - - - - - - - - - - - - - - - - -

_____

_____

- - - - - - - - - - - - - - - - - - - -

_____

_____

- - - - - - - - - - - - - - - - - - - -

_____

Name _____

Guided close Reading

Closely reread the list that Toad writes on the paper at the beginning of "A List" (page 6).

Directions: Think about these questions. In the chart, write ideas or draw pictures as you think. Be ready to share your answers.

❶ Use the list to describe what Toad is going to do today.

❷ What text from the list supports that Toad and Frog are friends?

❸ Which things on the list match what you might do on a Saturday?

Name _____

Making connections—"To Do" List

Directions: Many people make lists. Lists help you to be organized. Make a list of everything you want to do tomorrow. Start with "Wake up." End with "Go to sleep."

TO DO List

- Wake up.

  _____

- -

  _____

  _____

- -

  _____

  _____

- -

  _____

  _____

- -

  _____

  _____

- -

  _____

- Go to sleep.

Name _____

Language Learning—Adjectives

Directions: Frog and Toad are best friends. What else do you know about them? Write at least three adjectives to tell about each character. Examples have been given for you.

Frog	Toad
smart	silly

Name _____

Story Elements—Setting

Directions: Draw a map of where "A List" takes place. Include these places:

- Toad's house
- Frog's house
- the hills
- the swamps
- the place where Frog and Toad fall asleep

Name _____

Story Elements—Plot

Directions: Write a list that tells what happens in the story. Include all the important events.

_____

- _ _ _ _ _ _ _ _ _ _ _ _ _ _ _ _ _
  _____
  _____

- _ _ _ _ _ _ _ _ _ _ _ _ _ _ _ _ _
  _____
  _____

- _ _ _ _ _ _ _ _ _ _ _ _ _ _ _ _ _
  _____
  _____

- _ _ _ _ _ _ _ _ _ _ _ _ _ _ _ _ _
  _____
  _____

- _ _ _ _ _ _ _ _ _ _ _ _ _ _ _ _ _
  _____
  _____

- _ _ _ _ _ _ _ _ _ _ _ _ _ _ _ _ _
  _____
  _____

- _ _ _ _ _ _ _ _ _ _ _ _ _ _ _ _ _
  _____

Vocabulary Overview

Key words and phrases from this section are provided below with definitions and sentences about how the words are used in the story. Introduce and discuss these important vocabulary words with students. If you think these words or other words in the story warrant more time devoted to them, there are suggestions in the introduction for other vocabulary activities (page 5).

Word	Definition	Sentence about Text
garden (pg. 18)	a piece of ground where plants are grown	Frog creates a **garden** by his house.
fine (pg. 18)	nice, pleasant	Toad describes Frog's garden as **fine**, or nice.
seeds (pg. 18)	something that grows into plants	Frog gives Toad flower **seeds** to plant in the ground.
plant (pg. 18)	to put seeds into the ground	Toad wants to **plant** the seeds and make his own garden.
quite (pg. 19)	really	Toad is hoping his garden will grow **quite** soon.
noise (pg. 22)	any type of sound	Toad makes a lot of **noise** yelling at his seeds because they are not growing.
afraid (pg. 22)	scared	Toad thinks his seeds might be **afraid** to grow.
shine (pg. 23)	to give off light	The sun will **shine** on the seeds to help them grow.
poems (pg. 26)	writing that is specially arranged	Toad reads **poems** to his seeds to keep them company.
frightened (pg. 27)	afraid or scared	Toad is afraid that his seeds are the most **frightened** seeds in the world.

Name _____

Vocabulary Activity

Directions: Draw lines to complete the sentences.

Beginnings of Sentences	Endings of Sentences
Frog's garden has	**poems** to his seeds.
At the beginning of the story, Frog is	many **plants**.
Toad reads	and asks what is making so much **noise**.
Frog comes to Toad's garden	**frightened** seeds in the world.
Toad thinks that he has the most	in his **garden**.

Directions: Answer this question.

1. What needs to **shine** on the seeds for them to grow?

_____

_ _ _ _ _ _ _ _ _ _ _ _ _ _ _ _ _ _ _

_____

Analyzing the Literature

Provided below are discussion questions you can use in small groups, with the whole class, or for written assignments. Each question is written at two levels so you can choose the right question for each group of students. For each question, a few key points are provided for your reference as you discuss the book with students.

Story Element	Level 1	Level 2	Key Discussion Points
Character	How do you know that Frog is a good friend?	In what ways does Frog support Toad in the story?	Frog gives seeds to Toad and encourages him. Frog tells Toad what the seeds really need. Frog shows Toad that his garden is starting to grow.
Character	Why does Toad yell at his seeds?	Describe how Toad is impatient with his seeds.	He expects his seeds to grow right away. Sometimes, important things take time and yelling doesn't make them come any faster.
Setting	What is a garden?	Describe the parts of a garden.	A garden is a place where you can put seeds in the ground and have them grow into plants. There are often rows of plants in a garden.
Plot and Science	What really causes the seeds to grow?	Why do the seeds eventually grow?	The seeds really grow because the sun shines on them, the rain waters them, and the soil feeds them.

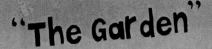

Name _____

Reader Response

Think

Think about gardening. Have you ever seen a garden in your neighborhood? Do you have your own garden?

Opinion Writing Prompt

Describe which garden you would rather have: a flower garden or a vegetable garden.

_____

_ _ _ _ _ _ _ _ _ _ _ _ _ _ _ _

_____

_____

_ _ _ _ _ _ _ _ _ _ _ _ _ _ _ _

_____

_____

_ _ _ _ _ _ _ _ _ _ _ _ _ _ _ _

_____

_____

_ _ _ _ _ _ _ _ _ _ _ _ _ _ _ _

_____

_____

_ _ _ _ _ _ _ _ _ _ _ _ _ _ _ _

_____

Name _____

Guided close Reading

Closely reread page 26, where Toad sings, reads, and plays music for his seeds.

Directions: Think about these questions. In the chart, write ideas or draw pictures as you think. Be ready to share your answers.

❶ Use the book to describe how Toad tries to help his seeds.

❷ What do you notice about the words in the three paragraphs on this page?

❸ Based on these events, what else could Toad try to do to help his seeds?

Name _____

Making connections— Singing Growing Songs

Toad wants his own garden. He is worried. The seeds aren't growing! He reads to them. Then, he sings to them. What song would you sing to seeds? Maybe it would be like this one.

Plant, Plant, Plant Your Seeds

(Sing to the tune of "Row, Row, Row Your Boat")

Plant, plant, plant your seeds—
Any type of seeds.
Add water, sunshine, some patience, and time—
This is all they need.

Directions: Make up your own seeds song.

_____

- -

_____
_____

- -

_____
_____

- -

_____
_____

- -

_____

Name _____

Language Learning—Dialogue

Directions: Write what you think Frog and Toad would say to each other.

" _____

_____

_____ ," says Frog.

Toad answers, " _____

_____ "

•

Frog says, " _____

_____ "

•

" _____

_____ ," answers Toad.

Name _____

Story Elements—
character and Setting

Directions: Think about the story "The Garden."
Answer the questions in sentences.

Question	Answer
Character Who is in the story?	
Setting Where does this story take place?	

Name _____

Story Elements—Plot

Directions: Write a poem about gardens. Maybe Toad could read it to his seeds.

_____

- - - - - - - - - - - - - - - -

_____

_____

- - - - - - - - - - - - - - - -

_____

_____

- - - - - - - - - - - - - - - -

_____

_____

- - - - - - - - - - - - - - - -

_____

Vocabulary Overview

Key words and phrases from this section are provided below with definitions and sentences about how the words are used in the story. Introduce and discuss these important vocabulary words with students. If you think these words or other words in the story warrant more time devoted to them, there are suggestions in the introduction for other vocabulary activities (page 5).

Word	Definition	Sentence about Text
cookies (pg. 30)	sweet, flat baked goods	Frog and Toad eat a lot of yummy **cookies** in this story.
baked (pg. 30)	cooked by dry heat	Before this story begins, Toad **baked** some cookies.
eaten (pg. 31)	to swallow food	When Frog thinks about it, he realizes that he has **eaten** too many cookies.
another (pg. 32)	a different one from the one before	Both Frog and Toad want **another** cookie.
reaching (pg. 34)	putting your hand out	Frog is **reaching** for a cookie as he talks about needing will power.
will power (pg. 34)	to control your behavior	**Will power** may be the only way to stop eating the cookies.
ladder (pg. 38)	steps for climbing up or down	Frog hopes that using a **ladder** to put the cookies up high will stop them from eating.
shelf (pg. 38)	a horizontal surface to hold things	Frog puts the cookies on a high **shelf**.
everywhere (pg. 40)	all around; different places	Birds want the cookies and come from **everywhere** to grab them.
beaks (pg. 40)	hard, pointed mouths of birds	The birds pick up the cookies in their **beaks**.

Name _____

Vocabulary Activity

Directions: These sentences are from the story written by Arnold Lobel. Cut apart the sentence strips. Put the sentences in order. Use the story to help you.

"These are the best cookies
I have ever **eaten**!" said Frog.

"We must stop eating!" cried
Toad as he ate **another**.

They picked up all the cookies
in their **beaks** and flew away.

"**These** cookies smell very
good," said Toad.

Birds came from **everywhere**.

Analyzing the Literature

Provided here are discussion questions you can use in small groups, with the whole class, or for written assignments. Each question is written at two levels so that you can choose the right question for each group of students. For each question, a few key points are provided for your reference as you discuss the book with students.

Story Element	Level 1	Level 2	Key Discussion Points
Plot	What is the problem in this story?	Describe the problem and solution in this story.	The problem is that Frog and Toad can't stop eating cookies! Frog tries many things to solve the problem, but finally he has to give the cookies away to stop eating.
Character	Why do Frog and Toad need will power?	Compare yourself to Frog and Toad in this story. When have you needed will power?	Students should discuss that the cookies are so good that Frog and Toad don't want to stop eating them. They have to make themselves stop, which means they need will power. Any comparisons students make are fine as long as they tie what they are saying back to the story.
Plot	What else could Frog and Toad have done with the cookies?	How else could Frog and Toad have saved the cookies?	Point out the various ways that Frog tries to put the cookies away. Discuss why the box, the shelf, and the string don't work.
Setting	What is the most interesting part of the setting of the book?	Describe the setting of the story.	The story takes place in Frog's house. The settings for the other stories in the book are in Toad's house or outside. This is the only time readers get to see the inside of Frog's house.

#40001—Instructional Guide: Frog and Toad Together   © Shell Education

Name _____

Reader Response

Think

Frog and Toad have a hard time controlling themselves. They want to keep eating the cookies. Think about a time when you couldn't control yourself.

Informative/Explanatory Writing Prompt

Describe what you do when you have to control yourself. What steps do you take to get control?

_____

- - - - - - - - - - - - - - - -

_____
_____

- - - - - - - - - - - - - - - -

_____
_____

- - - - - - - - - - - - - - - -

_____
_____

- - - - - - - - - - - - - - - -

_____
_____

- - - - - - - - - - - - - - - -

_____

Name _____

Guided close Reading

Closely reread from where Frog gives coookies to the birds through the end of the story (pages 40–41).

Directions: Think about these questions. In the chart, write ideas or draw pictures as you think. Be ready to share your answers.

❶ What words in the story show you how Toad feels about the birds eating the cookies?

❷ Based on the text and pictures, how do you know if the birds like the cookies?

❸ Use the text to describe what Toad is going to do next.

Name _____

Making connections—
chocolate chip Math!

Directions: Frog and Toad love cookies. Toad is a very good baker. He also likes math. When he bakes, he uses math! See if you can help Toad solve these math problems.

1. Toad makes 5 cookies. Each cookie needs 5 chocolate chips. How many chocolate chips does Toad need?

   _____

   _ _ _ _ _ _ _ _ _ _ _ _ _ _ _ _

   _____

2. Toad has 15 chocolate chips to make cookies. Frog eats 5 of these chocolate chips. How many chocolate chips does Toad have left?

   _____

   _ _ _ _ _ _ _ _ _ _ _ _ _ _ _ _

   _____

3. Toad needs 20 chocolate chips to make cookies. He only has 15. How many more does he need?

   _____

   _ _ _ _ _ _ _ _ _ _ _ _ _ _ _ _

   _____

Name _____

Language Learning—Agreement

Directions: Fill in the blank for each sentence. Write the verb that matches each subject.

1. Frog eats cookies.

_____

- - - - - - - - - - - - - -

Frog and Toad _____ cookies.

(eat *or* eats)

• •

2. Birds hop on the ground.

_____

- - - - - - - - - - - - - -

The bird _____ on the ground.

(hop *or* hops)

• •

3. Frog and Toad hide the cookies.

_____

- - - - - - - - - - - - - -

Frog _____ the cookies.

(hide *or* hides)

Name _____

Story Elements—Plot

Directions: Fill in what happened next.

Toad bakes some cookies.

_____
- - - - - - - - - - - - - - - - -
_____
_____
_____
- - - - - - - - - - - - - - - - -
_____

Frog puts the cookies in a box.

_____
- - - - - - - - - - - - - - - - -
_____
_____
- - - - - - - - - - - - - - - - -
_____
_____
_____

Name _____

Story Elements—Characters

Directions: Draw a picture of you, Frog, and Toad eating cookies.

Vocabulary Overview

Key words and phrases from this section are provided below with definitions and sentences about how the words are used in the story. Introduce and discuss these important vocabulary words with students. If you think these words or other words in the story warrant more time devoted to them, there are suggestions in the introduction for other vocabulary activities (page 5).

Word	Definition	Sentence about Text
dragon (pg. 42)	a mythological creature that breathes fire	Frog and Toad are reading a book where people fight **dragons**.
giant (pg. 42)	a very large person	The people fighting **giants** are never afraid.
brave (pg. 42)	having courage; not showing fear	Frog and Toad wonder if they are **brave**.
afraid (pg. 42)	full of fear	Frog and Toad do not think the characters in the story are **afraid**.
mirror (pg. 42)	a polished surface that shows a reflection	Frog and Toad look at themselves in a **mirror** to see if they are brave.
leaping (pg. 44)	jumping	Frog goes **leaping** over rocks.
puffing (pg. 44)	breathing heavily	Toad is **puffing** up behind Frog.
shaking (pg. 45)	moving up and down quickly	Toad is **shaking** when he sees the big snake.
avalanche (pg. 46)	many rocks and stones sliding down a hill	Many stones roll down the hill in an **avalanche**.
trembling (pg. 47)	shaking with fear or cold	Frog is **trembling** after the avalanche.

Name _____

Vocabulary Activity

Directions: Complete each sentence below. Use the words in the list.

Words from the Story

dragons	giants	brave	afraid	mirror
leaping	puffing	shaking	avalanche	trembling

1. Toad thinks the people in the book are

   _____.

2. When Frog and Toad jump away from the snake,

   Toad is _____.

3. Frog and Toad think they are not _____!

4. On the way up the mountain, Frog goes

   _____ over the rocks.

Directions: Answer this question.

5. What is something in the story that makes Frog and
   Toad **afraid**?

   _____

   _

   _____

   _

   _____

Analyzing the Literature

Provided below are discussion questions you can use in small groups, with the whole class, or for written assignments. Each question is written at two levels so you can choose the right question for each group of students. For each question, a few key points are provided for your reference as you discuss the book with students.

Story Element	Level 1	Level 2	Key Discussion Points
Character	Frog and Toad are reading together. What do you do with your friends?	Compare yourself and your best friend to Frog and Toad.	The discussion should focus on making connections between their lives and the characters in the book.
Setting	Describe where this story takes place.	This setting is more diverse than other Frog and Toad stories. Describe what is different about this setting.	The other Frog and Toad stories in this book take place near the characters' houses. This story allows students to see other parts of the world where Frog and Toad live.
Plot	What is the most exciting part of the story?	What is the problem in this story and how is it solved?	Students may point out the problem as Frog and Toad facing scary challenges. Staying together and returning to their familiar setting solves the problem.
Character	Describe whether you think Frog and Toad are brave.	In what ways are Frog and Toad brave in this story?	Although the story leads you to laugh at Frog and Toad for their fear, there are also ways that the characters are brave. They climb a mountain. They approach a dark cave. They face an avalanche.

Name _____

Reader Response

Think

Think about what makes you nervous. What are you scared of in your home or neighborhood?

Narrative Writing Prompt

Write about a time that you were scared. What did you do to feel better?

_____

_____

_____

_____

_____

_____

_____

_____

_____

_____

_____

_____

Guided close Reading

Closely reread the last two pages of the story where Frog and Toad hide in Toad's house (pages 50–51).

Directions: Think about these questions. In the chart, write ideas or draw pictures as you think. Be ready to share your answers.

❶ Use the text to tell why the readers may think that Frog and Toad are NOT brave.

❷ What words help you understand how Frog and Toad are feeling?

❸ In what ways do Frog and Toad help each other?

Name _____

Making connections—Animals

Directions: Frog and Toad meet two different animals in this story. They meet a snake. Then, they meet a hawk. List some other animals that Frog and Toad could meet on a walk.

Big Animals	Small Animals
deer	squirrel

Language Learning—
Rewriting Sentences

Directions: Below are some sentences. **Choose one.** Add new words to make the sentence better. Write your new sentence on the lines below. Then, draw a picture to make your sentence come alive.

Toad is brave.	Giants are big.
Frog likes hiking.	Rocks fall.

_____

_ _

_____

_ _

_____

Name _____

Story Elements—Plot

Directions: The events in a story are part of the plot. Fill in the missing events from this story.

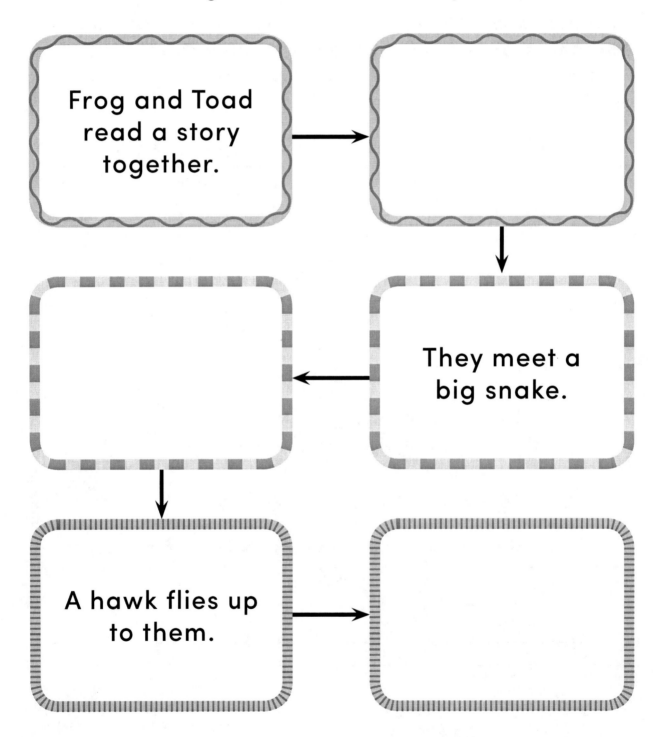

Frog and Toad read a story together.

They meet a big snake.

A hawk flies up to them.

Name _____

Story Elements—characters

Directions: Draw pictures of the big snake and the hawk. Instead of making them mean and scary, make them nice. In your picture, show the animals as kind and helpful.

Vocabulary Overview

Key words and phrases from this section are provided below with definitions and sentences about how the words are used in the story. Introduce and discuss these important vocabulary words with students. If you think these words or other words in the story warrant more time devoted to them, there are suggestions in the introduction for other vocabulary activities (page 5).

Word	Definition	Sentence about Text
dream (pg. 52)	mental images in your head when you're asleep	Toad is having a **dream** for most of this story.
stage (pg. 52)	a flat place where performers stand to be seen by an audience	In his dream, Toad is on a **stage**.
theater (pg. 52)	a building for performances	Toad's stage is in a **theater** with lots of seats.
strange (pg. 53)	not normal	The voice Toad hears is very **strange** and far away.
presenting (pg. 53)	introducing	The strange voice is **presenting** Toad to the audience.
bow (pg. 54)	to bend at the waist	As he begins, Toad takes a deep **bow**.
hooray (pg. 54)	good job	Frog shouts, "**Hooray** for Toad!"
high wire (pg. 56)	a rope high above the ground	Toad walks on a **high wire**.
peeped (pg. 57)	high-pitched sound	Frog is so little that he **peeps** when he talks.
lonely (pg. 60)	without friends	Toad realizes that he will be very **lonely** without Frog.

Name _____

Vocabulary Activity

Directions: Write at least two sentences using words from the story.

Words from the Story

dream	stage	theater	strange	presenting
bow	hooray	high wire	peeps	lonely

_____

_____

_____

_____

_____

_____

_____

_____

_____

Directions: Answer this question.

1. How is Toad's **dream strange**?

_____

_____

_____

_____

Analyzing the Literature

Provided below are discussion questions you can use in small groups, with the whole class, or for written assignments. Each question is written at two levels so that you can choose the right question for each group of students. For each question, a few key points are provided for your reference as you discuss the book with students.

Story Element	Level 1	Level 2	Key Discussion Points
Character	Why does Toad dream about being onstage?	Describe what Toad's dream tells us about Toad.	Toad likes to be the center of attention. Most Frog and Toad stories are about Toad. Maybe Toad realizes that he gets more attention than Frog.
Character	How would you feel if you were Frog from Toad's dream?	Compare how Frog feels in the dream with a time in your life when you've felt the same way.	Students should discuss what the phrase "feeling small" means and how it relates to this story.
Setting	Describe the setting of this story.	How is this setting different from the other Frog and Toad stories?	The stage is a very different setting for a Frog and Toad book. The end, which takes place in Toad's bedroom, is the traditional setting of most Frog and Toad stories.
Plot	How do you know that Frog is a good friend in this story?	What does the line, "'I always do,' said Frog," mean to you?	Frog is always there to support Toad, even when Toad is selfish. Frog seems more like a big brother who takes care of Toad than just a friend.

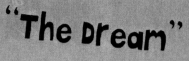

Name _____

Reader Response

Think

Think about who your best friends are. What do they like to do for fun? Why do you like them so much?

Informative/Explanatory Writing Prompt

Write about your best friends. Describe the reasons you like to play with them.

_____

- - - - - - - - - - - - - - - - - - - -

_____

- - - - - - - - - - - - - - - - - - - -

_____

- - - - - - - - - - - - - - - - - - - -

_____

- - - - - - - - - - - - - - - - - - - -

_____

- - - - - - - - - - - - - - - - - - - -

_____

- - - - - - - - - - - - - - - - - - - -

_____

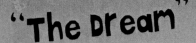

Name _____

Guided close Reading

Closely reread the two pages where Toad realizes Frog is gone (pages 59–60). Start at "There was no answer." Stop after "'I will be lonely!'"

Directions: Think about these questions. In the chart, write ideas or draw pictures as you think. Be ready to share your answers.

❶ What part of the text helps you understand how Toad is feeling?

❷ What other stories show you how Toad feels about Frog?

❸ Use the text to tell where you think Frog has gone.

Name _____

Making connections—BFFs!

Directions: Think about what makes a good friend. Label this body outline with everything you like in a friend. For each label, draw a line to the right body part. See the example below. Include at least four new ideas.

Says nice things. _____

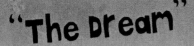

Name _____

Language Learning—Exclamations!

Directions: Write at least three sentences about the story. Each one must end with an exclamation point.

_____

- -

_____

- -

_____

- -

_____

- -

_____

- -

_____

- -

_____

Name _____

Story Elements—Character

Directions: Pick either Frog or Toad. Draw a picture of how his face looks at four different parts of the story. Label each picture.

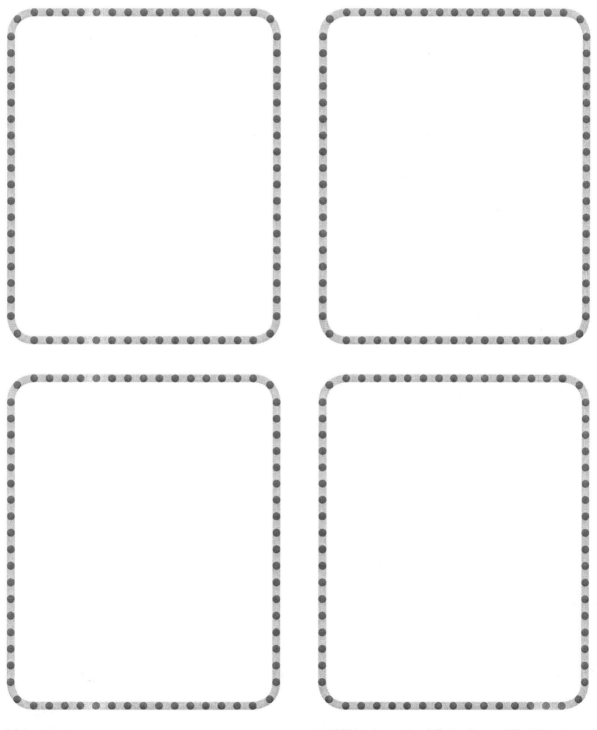

Name _____

Story Elements—Plot

Directions: Draw a picture of a stage with you on it. You can be playing the piano. Or, maybe you are walking on a high wire. You can even be dancing in your picture.

Post-Reading Theme Thoughts

Directions: Pretend you are Frog or Toad. Draw a picture of a happy face or a sad face for each statement. Then, use words to explain how the character feels.

Character I Chose _____

Statement	How Do You Feel? ☺ ☹	Explain How Frog or Toad Feels
Best friends should help each other.		
It is important to be patient. That means you have to wait for good things to happen.		
Sometimes you have to stop doing something you love.		
You have to be brave when you're scared.		

#40001—*Instructional Guide: Frog and Toad Together*

Culminating Activity: Your Own Adventures!

Directions: Work with students to help them choose one of the following activities. Most likely, these activities will require adult assistance to complete. The masks on pages 62–63 may be fun for students to use as they perform these different activities. Also included, on page 61, are figures for Frog and Toad in case students want to use these in their activities.

Write and draw your own Frog and Toad adventure. Base the story on your own experiences with a friend. For example, you could write "Frog and Toad on the Monkey Bars," "Frog and Toad at Soccer Practice," or "Frog and Toad at the Sleepover." Use the masks on pages 62–63 to perform your script.

Work with an adult or a few friends to write a reader's theater script. In the script, write a new Frog and Toad adventure. Then, use the masks on pages 62–63 to perform your script. If you want, you can make sock puppets instead of using the masks. (Dye socks different shades of green and brown and add googly eyes.)

Use clay and other materials (twigs, leaves, construction paper, etc.) to recreate scenes from the book. Take photographs of the clay scenes. Then, make your own Frog and Toad book with these new pictures.

Culminating Activity:
Your Own Adventures! *(cont.)*

culminating Activity:
Your own Adventures! *(cont.)*

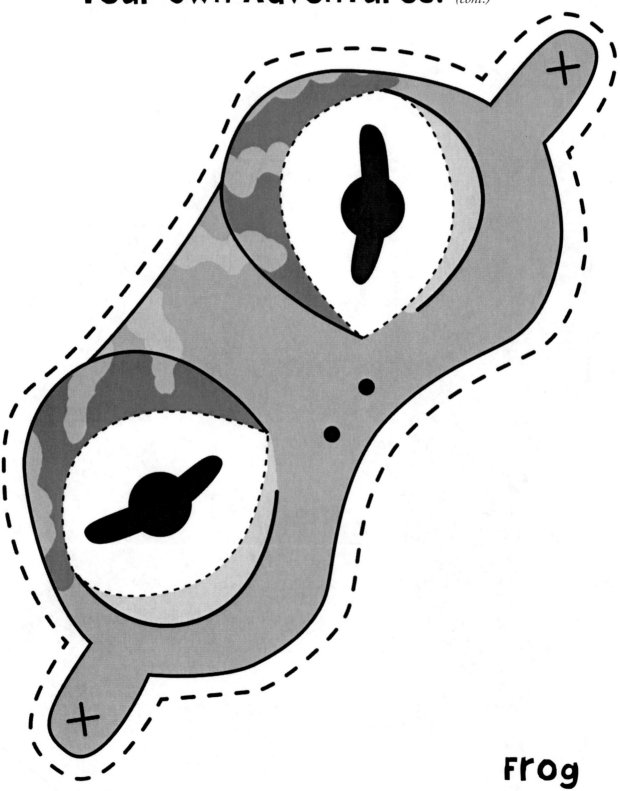

frog

culminating Activity:
Your own Adventures! *(cont.)*

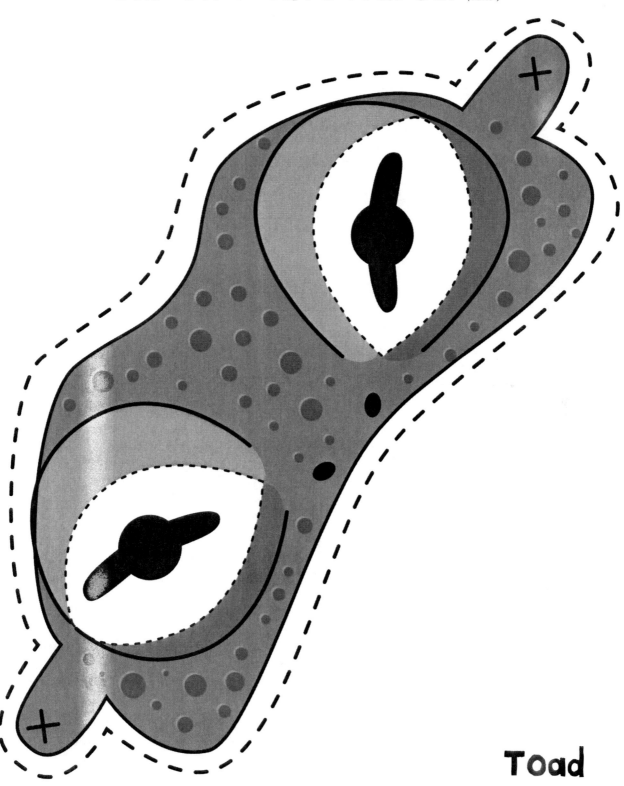

Toad

Name _____

comprehension Assessment

Directions: Fill in the bubble for the best response to each question.

"A List"

1. What shows Frog being a good friend?

   (A) Toad is at Frog's front door.

   (B) The wind blows the list out of Toad's hand.

   (C) Frog runs after the list.

   (D) Toad sits and does nothing.

"The Garden"

2. Why does Toad yell at his seeds?

   (A) His seeds do not grow right away.

   (B) His seeds are being too noisy.

   (C) His seeds will not listen.

   (D) His seeds are plants already.

"cookies"

3. What shows that Toad does not have will power?

   (A) "Toad baked some cookies."

   (B) "'You are right,' said Toad."

   (C) "Frog got a ladder."

   (D) "'We must stop eating!' cried Toad as he ate another."

comprehension Assessment *(cont.)*

"Dragons and Giants"

4. Describe how Frog and Toad are brave in this story.

_____

- -

_____

- -

_____

- -

_____

- -

_____

"The Dream"

5. What shows that Frog is very important to Toad?

- (A) "'Frog, can you be as wonderful as this?' said Toad."
- (B) "'Come back, Frog,' he shouted."
- (C) "'I always do,' said Frog."
- (D) "Toad took a deep bow."

Name _____

Response to Literature: Describing Friendship

Directions: Choose one scene from any of the Frog and Toad stories you've read. Think about which scene is your favorite. Draw a picture of that scene. Then, answer the questions on the next page about your scene. Make sure your picture is neat and is in color.

Response to Literature: Describing Friendship (cont.)

1. What is happening in the scene?

_____

- - - - - - - - - - - - - - - - - -

_____
_____

- - - - - - - - - - - - - - - - - -

_____

2. Why did you choose this scene?

_____

- - - - - - - - - - - - - - - - - -

_____
_____

- - - - - - - - - - - - - - - - - -

_____

3. What happens next in the story?

_____

- - - - - - - - - - - - - - - - - -

_____
_____

- - - - - - - - - - - - - - - - - -

_____

Name _____

Response to Literature Rubric

Directions: Use this rubric to evaluate student responses to their Describing Friendship activity.

Great Job	Good Work	Keep Trying
☐ You answered all three questions completely. You included many details.	☐ You answered all three questions.	☐ You did not answer all three questions.
☐ Your handwriting is very neat. There are no spelling errors.	☐ Your handwriting can be neater. There are some spelling errors.	☐ Your handwriting is not very neat. There are many spelling errors.
☐ Your picture is neat and fully colored.	☐ Your picture is neat and some of it is colored.	☐ Your picture is not very neat and/or fully colored.
☐ Creativity is clear in both the picture and the writing.	☐ Creativity is clear in either the picture or the writing.	☐ There is not much creativity in either the picture or the writing.

Teacher Comments: _____

_____

_____

_____

Name _____

_____

- - - - - - - - - - - - - - - - - -

_____

_____

- - - - - - - - - - - - - - - - - -

_____

_____

- - - - - - - - - - - - - - - - - -

_____

_____

- - - - - - - - - - - - - - - - - -

Name _____

_____

- -

_____

- -

_____

- -

_____

- -

_____

- -

_____

- -

_____

- -

_____

The responses provided here are just examples of what students may answer. Many accurate responses are possible for the questions throughout this unit.

Vocabulary Activity—Section 1: "A List" (page 15)
1. Toad loses his **list** in this story.

Guided Close Reading—Section 1: "A List" (page 18)
1. Toad is planning to get up, eat breakfast, get dressed, go to Frog's house, go on a walk, eat lunch, take a nap, play with Frog, eat supper, and go to sleep.
2. Toad is planning to go to Frog's house, take a walk with Frog, and play games with Frog.
3. Students need to reference the list when they talk about their weekend plans.

Vocabulary Activity—Section 2: "The Garden" (page 24)

- At the beginning of the story, Frog is in his garden.
- Toad reads poems to his seeds.
- Frog comes to Toad's garden and asks what is making so much noise.
- Toad thinks that he has the most frightened seeds in the world.
1. Sun needs to **shine** on the seeds for them to grow.

Guided Close Reading—Section 2: "The Garden" (page 27)
1. Toad tries to help his seeds by singing songs. He also reads poems. Finally, he plays music for his seeds.
2. The words in the three paragraphs on this page are almost the same. Only the verb and the word after are different (sang songs, read poems, and played music).
3. Students' responses should relate to the three things Toad does on this page. For example, Toad could try to help his seeds by writing a story about them. Or maybe Toad could put on a play for the seeds.

Story Elements—Section 2: "The Garden" (page 30)

Who is in the story?	Frog and Toad are characters in this story.
Where does this story take place?	The story takes place in Frog's garden and in Toad's garden.

Vocabulary—Section 3: "Cookies" (page 33)

- "These **cookies** smell very good," said Toad.
- "These are the best cookies I have ever **eaten**!" said Frog.
- "We must stop eating!" cried Toad as he ate **another**.
- Birds came from **everywhere**.
- They picked up all the cookies in their **beaks** and flew away.

Guided Close Reading—Section 3: "Cookies" (page 36)
1. Toad feels sad about the birds eating the cookies. "'Now we have no more cookies to eat,' said Toad sadly. 'Not even one.'"
2. The birds look happy in the pictures. The birds took all the cookies in their beaks.
3. Toad is going to go home and "bake a cake."

Making Connections—Section 3: "Cookies" (page 37)
1. $5 + 5 + 5 + 5 + 5 = 25$ chocolate chips
2. $15 - 5 = 10$ chocolate chips
3. $20 - 15 = 5$ chocolate chips

Language Learning—Section 3: "Cookies" (page 38)
1. Frog and Toad **eat** cookies.
2. The bird **hops** on the ground.
3. Frog **hides** the cookies.

Story Elements—Section 3: "Cookies" (page 39)

Toad bakes some cookies. → He eats a cookie and loves it.

Frog puts the cookies in a box. → Toad points out that they can just open the box.

Vocabulary Activity—Section 4:
"Dragons and Giants" (page 42)

1. Toad thinks the people in the book are **brave**.

2. When Frog and Toad jump away from the snake, Toad is **shaking**.

3. Frog and Toad think they are not **afraid**!

4. On the way up the mountain, Frog goes **leaping** over the rocks.

5. Frog and Toad are **afraid** of the snake, the avalanche, and the hawk.

Guided Close Reading—Section 4:
"Dragons and Giants" (page 45)

1. Toad is not brave because he pulls "the covers over his head." Frog is not brave because he jumps into the closet and shuts the door. "They stayed there for a long time." That doesn't sound very brave either.

2. The following words help you understand how Frog and Toad are feeling: jumped, pulled, brave, shut, stayed, and together.

3. Frog and Toad help each other by telling each other that they are brave. It feels good to hear a friend tell them that they are brave.

Story Elements—Section 4:
"Dragons and Giants" (page 48)

- Frog and Toad read a story together.
- **They decide to climb a mountain.**
- They meet a big snake.
- **They see an avalanche.**
- A hawk flies up to them.
- **They run home and hide.**

Vocabulary Activity —Section 5:
"The Dream" (page 51)

1. Toad's **dream** is **strange** because he is doing very weird things on a stage. Also, he is being very boastful to Frog, and that is not something that happens when Toad is awake.

Guided Close Reading—Section 5:
"The Dream" (page 54)

1. The look on Toad's face in the pictures tell the reader a lot about how he is feeling. The words "'Frog, what have I done?' cried Toad" make you realize that Toad is upset. Also, Toad screams at the strange voice. Finally, Toad shouts, "I will be lonely!"

2. Toad and Frog are best friends. Be sure students reference other Frog and Toad stories to support their opinions.

3. Frog has disappeared. It says, "Frog was so small that he could not be seen or heard." So, Frog became so unimportant in the dream that he actually disappeared right out of the dream.

Comprehension Assessment (page 64)

1. C. Frog runs after the list.

2. A. His seeds do not grow right away.

3. D. "'We must stop eating!' cried Toad as he ate another."

4. Frog and Toad are brave in this story in some ways. They decide to climb a mountain together. That is pretty brave. They keep going after they are almost eaten by a huge snake. They keep going even after an avalanche almost gets them. They succeed in reaching the top of the mountain.

5. B. "'Come back, Frog,' he shouted."